IN-GRATITUDE
AND
OTHER POEMS

For Michael & Karen
Warmest Wishes

Neville

IN-GRATITUDE
AND
OTHER POEMS

Neville Symington

KARNAC

First published in 2010 by
Karnac Books Ltd
118 Finchley Road
London NW3 5HT

British Library Cataloguing in Publication Data

A C.I.P. for this book is available from the British Library

ISBN-13: 978-1-85575-823-0

Typeset by Vikatan Publishing Solutions (P) Ltd., Chennai, India

Printed in Great Britain

www.karnacbooks.com

For My Mother and Father

CONTENTS

INTRODUCTION

I have often heard people being recommended to reflect on experience. For me the word reflect is too passive a counsel. Experience is the raw material that I need not just to reflect upon but to create into an art form. An insight which changed my whole way of thinking is when I read the statement from Giambattista Vico's *Nuova Scienza* that we only truly know that which we have created. It was a startling discovery because I now knew that I would only come to know, even my own experience, if I created it. I had to create what was already there; create it into an art form. There is no doubt that I know it when I have created it in a way which I did not know beforehand. It is what often holds me back from giving expression to something because, once I have done so, it changes that which was. Paul Tillich expresses it in this way:

> *Man, as finite freedom, is free within the contingencies of his finitude. But within these limits he is asked to make of himself what he is supposed to become, to fulfil his destiny, to the actualization of what he potentially is.*[1]

---

[1] Tillich, Paul. (1964). *The Courage to Be.* p. 58. Collins: The Fontana Library.

" ... *he is asked to make of himself what he is supposed to become.*" A mysterious sentence. That strange paradox that our life's task is to become who we are. Different thinkers have tried to give expression to this mysterious truth. Vico I have already mentioned. The psycho-analyst, Wilfred Bion, formulated the idea of *alpha function*—something in the personality that creates what is there into the art form of dreams. This is the way I like to think about it: creation of what is there.

Creation and communication are partners. When I communicate I am at the same time creating. Again Wilfred Bion distinguished between speech which is a discharge and speech which is a communication. The fact that someone speaks something to me does not mean that it is a communication; it can be a solipsistic discharge. A middle-aged man visited a psycho-analyst daily for a period of years. At the beginning of each session he said,

> 'You know, Doctor, I am very guilty about all sexual things.'

The psycho-analyst felt certain that this man knew that he was guilty about all sexual things. He said it repeatedly to the analyst. The analyst felt bored by the monotonous tone in which it was said. One day he came to the analyst's consulting-room and said,

> "Doctor, an amazing thing has happened to me to-day. I was shaving
> and looking at myself in the mirror and suddenly I realized that I am
> very guilty about sexual things."

There was life and energy behind his words and the analyst was not bored at all by what he was saying. On the previous days, weeks and months this man had been discharging but to-day, call it the day of the shaving mirror, he was communicating. The analyst made this reconstruction. The man, his patient, had had several previous therapeutic treatments. It is likely that previous therapists had said to him in a benign way and perhaps wanting to sympathise with his preoccupation: *you know you are very guilty about sexual things* but these had just gone in and sat like inert wooden blocks in his mind but on the day of the shaving mirror he created them and what was then expressed was a communication and not a discharge.

Tolstoy, in his essay *What is Art?*, goes through the aesthetic theories starting with Baumgarten. His conclusion that all these theories can be summarised either as seeing beauty as the expression of the infinite within the finite or that which pleases the senses and having no utilitarian qualities. He dismisses all these and says that art is communication and I find his definition entirely convincing. This means then that communication is a creation. When I want to communicate it puts the demand upon me to create what is inside me into an art form. There is, of course, much poetry, art and literature which is discharge or derivative. We need an inner creator to make the distinction between these two.

My life has been studded with numerous rich experiences. I have been lucky in that a day has never passed in which some enlightening happening has not occurred. It takes an effort to create these experiences into an art form. The fact that for the majority of my living time I have not been able to summon the effort to create tells me that I have been depressed all my life. Sometimes this is referred to as a 'functional depression'—in other words that inner spirit has been subdued into servitude to 'cultural normality'. Just occasionally I have been moved to create into poetry experiences which have hammered so insistently at my door that in the end I have had to come out of my torpor and create.

Where does the creative act come from? No one knows. All the rash of literature in recent times from artists, scientists and theologians on the subject of consciousness finds its origin in this puzzle.

Creating what has happened to one into an art form has one effect: it dissolves the barrier between the present and the past. The past is constantly stimulated into life by present experiences—particularly when listening to someone else relating their experiences. It brings me then into a close sharing of experience with the other. Analytic theories are substitutes for these personal experiences.

So these poems are a few casual glimpses when the spirit has risen to the challenge. They are not a big offering but they mean a lot to me. The most important of these is the long poem *IN-GRATITUDE* which comes first. It is the creation of some enormously important conversations I had with my mother shortly before she died.

IN-GRATITUDE

Introduction

I was fifty-six when this poem was written and, as is clear, it is about a week of conversations with my mother shortly before she died. They were the most important conversations I ever had with her and wronght a huge change in me and, I believe, were extremely important to her. I wrote down the conversations after each visit as close to verbatim as possible. About two years later I transformed them into this poem. In addition to the things we actually said to each other I also included in the poem some of my own self-reflections.

I have put this poem among the section of poems of childhood and put it first because my mother gave birth to me and suckled me as a baby and the whole of my life is inferred in this amazing dialogue that occurred between us. There is a tendency in the mental health world to blame mothers for one's misfortune. There is also a belief that one has a right to one's mother's love. I think these 'rights' which people believe belongs to them is the cause of much resentment and unhappiness in the world. Bob Gosling, who was

1

Chairman at the Tavistock Clinic for ten years from the mid-seventies to mid-eighties wrote the following in a letter to me:

> *In my view what gave me life, or at least saved me from death, is the amazing fact that my mother had inborn tendencies to minister to my infant helplessness and that they were sufficiently supported socially and culturally for her to work the miracle. From my point of view this was a totally unmerited gift—Grace, in fact. Ave Maria! So the choices we have to make everyday now in so far as they are very derived or developed forms of this first relationship depend on how much we can acknowledge and honour this Gift (and become identified with it).[1]*

We live in a culture where everyone is always clamouring about their rights. G.K. Chesterton who was one of the heroes of my youth said,

> *"A whole generation has been taught to talk nonsense at the top of its voice about having 'a right to life' and 'a right to experience' and 'a right to happiness.'"[2]*

I am deeply grateful to my mother and my father for the love that they showered upon me from my earliest years and right through their lives. My mother wrote to me nearly every week of my life when I was apart from her. It was such a joy when I was at school to see the envelope with the familiar sloping handwriting, then the same later when I was locked away in theological college. Her letters were always full of news of family and friends. She was a wonderful correspondent. I am only sorry that I did not keep her letters.

One of the great human puzzles is what is it that can change one from meanness to generosity, from ingratitude to gratitude, from blame to forgiveness? I think these possibilities do lie in our heart but that we need some powerful event to shake our miserable natures and root our being in these treasures that lie hidden in us. Tolstoy understood this very well. In his superb novel *Anna Karenina* Karenin is journeying from St. Petersburg back to his home in Moscow where his wife Anna was dying and had just given birth to a son whose

---

[1] Unpublished personal letter.
[2] Chesterton, G.K. (1938). *Autobiography.* p. 335. London: Hutchinson & Co.

father was Vronsky and not Karenin. Karenin was hoping while journeying towards home that Anna would die but when he saw her and the little baby, his heart melted and Tolstoy says of him:

"... it was not until he saw his dying wife that he knew his own heart."[3]

I think something similar happened to me in that precious week when I was with my mother before she died. It must mean that there was a generosity and gratitude inside me but it had become spoiled with cancerous spores that had infused them with indignant self-righteousness. Karenin's pride was wounded when Anna revealed her sexual affair with Vronsky. My pride was wounded when ... It took the event described in the poem for me to know my own heart. This deeper knowledge 'worked the miracle' and banished for ever that sour resentment.

---

[3] Tolstoy, L.N. (1986). *Anna Karenin*. p. 444. (Translated by Rosemary Edmonds). Penguin Books.

In-Gratitude

I started with some pleasantries
'How are you feeling, Mum?'
It was absurd to say it
For sighs and heavy breathing
And groggy speech spoke death.

My days were full of business then
Of self-important men.
Visits to my Mum were squeezed
Between lunch and consultation
Until a deeper rumbling sounded.

A groan was speaking deeply
Smothered 'neath this social haste
I rushed them through my brain
With chairman-like efficiency
And across my friendly Julian.

But Julian echoed depths
Of mother's death he told;
Regret he'd never asked her
'Is there nought you want to say?'
And he looked me in the eye.

You can see I wished I'd done it;
The chance is in your lap,
'I'm returning to Australia, Mum,
Is there nought you want to say
Before I fly across the globe?'

The truth of Julian's words
Could not be pushed away
His voice I had to follow
And practicalities were dead
With chairman in the grave.

A light now beamed on Julian;
Transformed - he's now my friend
His closeness to me now
Counted not by watch or body
But by echoes in the depths.

A person enters life
A brief encounter if you like
Yet it is a beam of light
Much greater than all meetings
Of my sunny social life.

In trembling fear but knowledge
That something good would come:
'Australia when I go there, Mum,
May be the last I see you.'
Her face suppressed some tears.

'I know I may be dead by then',
She spoke direct and true.
A nervous smile upon her lips
She looked me in the eyes
Which made the point eternal.

My words had voiced a favoured thought
T'was clearly on her mind.
She had been thinking long on it.
The daring instant brought right out
Our souls to trusting harmony.

Those awe-filled words did split
A chest of moving memories
Stretched back to earliest days.
The key disclosing life's own throb;
Might've stayed within my chest.

What is the fear of speaking words?
So simple on the written page
Yet having power to crack the heart
And open souls to love or hate
Or just appalling emptiness?

A great abyss would open deep
And chasmèd each on either side
Cracked icebergs parting on the seas
And safe protection lost for good
Replaced instead with spirits bound.

Each moment's now eternity.
Passing beyond our present sense
And stamped with spirit infinite
That passes through her life and mine
Stands warden of redeeme'd time.

A new era opens up for both
Abiding there since early years
But never voiced til near to death
A secret life within the depths
Is clearly there for each to know.

Is depth too much for daily life?
That only crisis can reveal?
That common parlance, jokes and chat
Is all that humans can embrace?
Emotion tides being kept for death?

And silence gave a place for thought,
No hurried words to stop a gap.
This whole new world into a womb
Of caring quiet that holds it all
And now all words were synchronous.

"Is there something I could do for you?
Like message to a friend or no?"
"Do something please for Susan Rumsey.
I cared for her a three years full
Adopted child she was to me.

So hard to mother other's child
What is right and what is wrong
Is easily judged for one's own
But judging for another's child
Is hard and painful - all unknown."

I felt a tear wetten my eye
So sad that she had kept this in
This burden hidden all these years
Unshared with Dad or Jill or James
And only now revealed to me.

She had so often wanted me
To be with her for company.
'Possessive Mum' my sour reply
Yet if I'd spoken laser words
The gates of silence would have parted.

I could have given something back
A tiny bit, minute I'd say
For all she gave and gave and gave
And never stopped through all my life
A tiny fraction could be repaid.

Within the Church the mother was
Placed upon a pedestal
And almost worshipped you might say.
I did my bidding as commanded
And worshipped her in frantic frenzy.

Then a saner view prevailed
The place of Mary overdone
A reformer's heart replaced the Catholic
Slowly was the mother spurned
From the high place of hitherto.

Analysis was Protestant
A ritual now of retribution.
Mum now went from bad to worse,
Jealous greed or envy rife
Filled all my mind from dawn to dusk.

A poison viper dwelt inside
Within my breast a hatred lay
Filled with venom and foul sludge
Hidden from the world around
It bred there like a parasite.

But own it in myself did I?
Not a thought of holy me
Harbouring such viciousness.
Envy, greed and jealousy
Belonged to others not to me.

And hated I these vices now
And there they were in her I say
Her very presence did I loathe
And wished her from my hideous sight
Obliterated from my view.

A loathsome sight she was to me
All blame was heaped upon her now
All the vicious things in me
I hated in her character
Loathing even kind affection.

Never was a son so bad
He hated his maternal flesh,
Lest we turn to oldest classics
Of Ancient Greece and find it there
In Agammemnon's fateful breast.

Did she turn in just revenge?
She kept this vileness all inside
Maintaining all her love for me
Not once rejecting me, her son
Or exacting retribution.

With this fierce expulsion now
I expelled to her all treasures too.
She held all these secure for me
Safer than a banker's trust
Returning them when I was ready.

This loathing was a passion now
So strong it now consumed my soul
And rotted all my faculties,
It lasted a dozen years at least
Corrupting my being's inwardness.

All this venon to her was pointed
Only aimed at her own person.
It was a madness of huge proportions.
Hidden from the world around
By keeping it in mother's safe.

Why did I point it all at her?
Her magnet now attracting it?
I knew she was the only one
To tolerate such viciousness
She would not divorce her younger son.

And I the little innocent
And analyst endorsed it all.
No doubt I egged him on apace.
It was a cure of my own soul
But only at her cruel expense.

This twisted vision of events
Believed by analyst entirely
I pulled the wool across his eyes
He treated me with warm compassion
Believing me, the maltreated one.

Harsh words I hear my colleagues say
Aghast to hear such strident words
Against a practice dear to them.
But dear to me as well I say
But let the truth reign first at last.

Let my tale a warning be
Lest others pull the wool as well
Making analysts a bunch of fools
Who join the blaming of our mothers
Failing to treat a rotten soul.

It is a cancer of the soul
Consuming lifeblood's sentiment
Hiding from the expert eye
Twisting truth to look a lie
And lying made to look like truth.

It is so nearly like the truth
But all the time so distant from it
It turns all what belongs to me
To an outer person close at hand
Like mother or a father now.

It's not our greed or envy too
It is its hatred in our breast
That is the wicked parasite.
To tolerate the bad in us
Can cure us of this vile disease.

Its presence is not mother's fault
Or father either for that matter.
It is not the fault of brother
Or sister or analyst or any other.
Its cause remains mysterious.

It is however love gone wrong.
Let mother take my ills in me
Sucking poison out of me
Aiding now the snake-bite victim
Taking it inside of her.

I was grown man to all my friends
But baby in my mother's eyes
The child's screams to mother went
To save me from this parasite.
She turned in love and did her bidding.

There's so much wrong with empathy
Divorced from mystic's vision
The Upanishads held to the truth
Of ultimate within the other
Yes there exactly there in mother.

A cure cannot be called a cure
Caring for my own precious soul
Neglecting now that ultimate
Residing close at hand to me
In my dear mother's loving soul.

Great wrong's been done with this delusion
And many's led astray the same
It is the illness of the age
Calling it my self-expression
Achieving my dearest self-fulfilment.

I hardly dare to think on it,
I groan with shame and hide my face
Beneath a welter of cliché phrases
Invented by that new disease:
That's called in aulas Social Science.

My eyes filled with freshly tears
Of the burden in her heart
Unimparted through the years
Carried in her loneliness
Not even shared with kith and kin.

She had not only hidden Susan
But her own son's cruel defection
This I now longed to undo
And give to her my love at last
Which she deserved from my own part.

'How did Susan come to stay?'
'She was living with her aunt
But was sore unhappy there
Her mother came and asked of me
To take her to our home instead.

She looked to distant years
'Such responsibility,' she said.
'What shall I do for her?' I said
'Could you invite her to your home?
She'd love swimming in your pool.'

Hidden tears welled up within
Seeing the unshared load instead
Carried in her secret breast
Down all those years of family life
We could have helped her with.

In families of closest ties
The worlds are hidden quite apart
From all of us and in each other.
A moment's glimpse sweeps back a veil
That does its job so very well.

The pain and treasures of within
Kept fortressed 'gainst perpetual storm
To open to our daily blood
Would tear our hearts in little shreds
And make of us damned invalids.

Mum kept it to the point of death
And then let open all her heart
Her love and generous pardon now
Were large and huge and pouring forth
To me in unemcumbered giving.

Love is such a dangerous thing
Opening emotion's arsenal
Regret and sorrow overwhelm me
Awareness is too much to bear
Of my own petty-mindedness.

* * *

There was a love-filled silence here
That brimmed two heartfuls to the top
Silence spoke with strength and power
Smothering stupid voices speech
Before I cut my words to her.

Now my thoughts found words at last
'When I left our mother Church
I would have died without your help,
I thank you now with all my heart
I cannot speak my gratitude.

She answered quick and firm to me:
'I hope so' were her simple words
'To bear the hatred of the cousins
When they bore their teeth at me
Was so hard for months on end.'

My own self-pity to my self
Had blinded me to naught but me
And my own precious suffering
Not a thought to her own pain
Did ever pass across my mind.

She suffered much on my behalf
Kept their sniping barbs within,
Never mentioning her own pain
Loyal to me through thick and thin
Knowing how her child was sick.

She was a mother very brave
Withstanding storms of pain and hurt
Her children she did fair defend
And cared for always valiantly
While silent of her searing pain.

She differed in her outer face
A merriness that brimmed with life
Rejoicing in life's joys a'full
Laughter hiding from the world
A hell of sorrow all within.

She drank and smoked and laughed a lot
Cheering us all along the path
Of life's grim journey to the grave
There was a sadness down within
That only us her children knew.

'Your children are all happy now;
Jill with Peter is content
And James with Penny too,
And I am lucky with my Joan
A wife to trust and more.'

Smiling joy she looked at me
With sparkling joy upon her face:
'That is so good for all of you,
I'm glad that Jill is married now
Living happily at last.'

'And what of you?' she wisely grinned.
A twinkling sadness in her eye'
'Are you settled now in life?'
'A bond of joy I've found in wife.
To trust for always through my life.'

'Though many rows we've had
And storms and windy seas
We do all love you from the depths
Without a doubt we all can say
We love you Mum and mean it fully'.

'I know it of you all that's true
And feel it often right in here'
She tapped her breast with gentle fist
To show to me now the place of it
And joy shone through her face awhile.

'We're happy in Australia land
The country of your distant birth.
Although we live so far from you
We're close in spirit all the day
And think together much of you.'

'We love the house beside the beach
With all the waves and surfing sound
We walk and frisk three miles of sand
We know how much you love the sea
And see you in the ocean breakers.

I knew she loved the beach and surf
Seeing Ozzie beaches in her mind.
She'd swum that sea through all her youth
And missed a shark's tooth by an inch
Being called the 'shark-bait' ever since.

It was a talk of trusty worth
You could rely with faith upon.
The truthful door once opened wide
Ushered in a rock sincere
Cementing life eternal now.

Next day I came embracing flowers
Her face was lit with cheerfulness:
"Thank you for your visits, dear
Each day to me in busy life.
I thank you now for all of it".

"I come because I want to come.
Love shrinks the world to golf-ball size
Each minute of this precious time
Is worth a year or even more
Of stupid aimless empty time."

I'll do for Susan all you asked.
What other favour can I do?"
Her brow was puckered into thought.
A touch of anguish in her breast.
Had she forgotten some dear friend?

'I hear Anthony's at Ancora now.'
Child's paradise was in my mind.
Its river where we swam as kids
Catching trouts for breakfast treat.
With Reg and Auriel indulging us.

Every summer there we went
And spent two weeks of merriment.
Walks and pic-nics during the day
And games and laughter in the night.
And seeing our parents happy too.

'Those were happy days,' I said,
'I loved those holidays so much.'
'They were such happy times,' she said.
Her mind fancied returning there
The scene of Ancora joined our hearts.

'And Canada? Was joy or strife?'
When I was baby child of three
Wrenched were we from sunny Porto
To weather years in Canada.
Escaping German tanks of war.

'Ripped was I from darling Ron
I could not even ring him then.
And he was badly ill you know
I could not reach across the ocean
To touch his near-death brow

'It was a most foreboding time
Would the war by us be won
Or plunged in darkness for an age
And never see my Ron again?
And you three children fatherless?'

'It was a time of darkest threat
And Canada a dire solution.
I could not at all enjoy it there
And was in hospital for months
Stiffening my knee for all my life.'

A stupid question I did ask,
Canada with Ancora joining
Was something like a sacrilege.
Mind images were blotted out
By my strangling arrogance.

'That leg did nuisance you a lot.'
'It was so painful too,' she said.
In all my life I had not known
A fact of all so obvious
Yet never once did mention it.

Her sister, Sheilagh, once did say:
'I think dear Norah suffers much
From that poor leg of hers always'
But these were only words to me,
To touch my heart I let them not.

I was enrapped within myself
Enclosed within a blinding cloak
That shuttered me from all the world
Especially from myself as well
Like some zombie along life's path.

And years of aimless introspection
With psycho-analysis as well
Had done naught at all to puncture it
This self-absorbed state that walked me
Trance-like through a life of fog.

There was a peaceful silence now
Of love touching a life between us
Enveloping the atmosphere.
It was a love that bred a calm
Embracing us the two in one.

'Viewing now your whole life long
Have you found a just fulfilment?
Or felt satisfied with all your years?'
Her answer came out soft and sadly:
'I can only say well 'Yes and No'.

It was a time to speak again
The words rolled from the atmosphere:
'I regret so much all my unkindness,
I'm sorry for so much of it.'
She looked at me a tranquil gaze.

The words that came were a surprise:
'I remember not the least unkindness.'
Words pouring from a generous heart.
I vowed I would repeat the sense
But with a more compelling force.

'Can you remember down the years
And see the baby in your arms?'
Her mind was searching life's horizon
Like stranded sailor seeing a ship.
'I remember very well,' she said.

'And even feeding me as well?'
'I remember feeding you myself
With my own breast-milk for a time
Then I gave you to Maria
You supped the bottle in my sight.'

'And Jill and James was it the same?
Can you remember them as well?'
'Yes, I remember feeding them
And watching them with bottles too
From Albertina's caring hands.

'My earliest memory, Mum, was you
Your leg upon a stool in plaster.'
She looked contentment in her eyes.
Those distant days were close to us
Right between us in the light.

'I remember being high up in flight
In plane from Lisbon to the States.
And looking o'er the billowing clouds
With fair-haired Alison close by.'
'It's funny what a child remembers.'

'Do you remember all that eczema?
All those creams and medicines too
That doctors tried to cure it with?'
'Yes, I remember all too well.'
'It's all gone now without a trace.'

'It's me who's got it now so bad.
It worries, itches, troubling me.'
'I am so sorry I did not know.'
'Don't worry, dear, I'm old you see
My aged skin is dry and cracked.'

All these aches and pains of life
Came out in this strange dialogue.
Hidden all these years from us
She now revealed them close to death.
It was a gift I now received.

I regretted deeply my neglect
But was so glad she let me know.
My heart went out to her in love
Even in her final hour it's not too late
To offer her a true contrition.

'Although we're in Australia now
Twelve thousand miles away from you.
You are so close to my own heart.
The place you have within my breast
Will never die for all my life.'

A new-found warmth flowed through the room
Her hand went to a handkerchief;
She dabbed her eyes and looked at me.
Her eyelids closed and brought her sleep
And peaceful dreams for her a while.

I sat in direst contemplation
What a task and where to start
To thank one's mother - for what I ask?
For everything from start to finish.
The debt it is too great to think.

A family once so dear to me
They took me in and cared for me
Their name was Carey as it chanced
And sheltered me for half a year
And brought me to my health again.

My gratitude to them is great
And Eila was a trusted friend
In time of sore dismemberment
With these and many others now
I can thank with full sincerity.

With these I knew where to begin
And where to finish gratitude.
Their gift though fully generous
Was for all its greatness circumscribed
With boundaries drawn around its girth.

But mother's gift is infinite.
Beyond powers of all imagining.
All the churches' songs of praise
Going heavenwards to saints and God
Are meant for earthly mothers here.

We are too mean to give them it
And give it to the Lord instead
Or else the movements in our breast
Would burst the floodgates of us all
And reduce us to a crying mess.

Or is this only poor excuse?
To cover our mean-heartedness?
I am not sure; I nothing know
Except that to my mother now
I owe a thanks that's infinite.

Attempting now to utter it
I'm puny and inadequate
No cowardly embarassment,
Will stop me now from doing it.
Even if it bursts my life.

To-morrow would be the day
The last before Australia death.
I would thank her for her motherhood
The words themselves mere empty vessels
Will fill up now with dire meaning.

The day had come; I entered in
She knew it was the final one.
Her mind was clear, her heart was large
She knew it was a death-like parting.
There's no deceit and all was clear.

'When does your plane leave here to-morrow?'
'It leaves at eleven in the morn'
'And when does it arrive?' she said.
'By England's time it will be morn
But evening on Austalia's clocks.'

Her brows did furrow in concentration
Determined to remember it.
She was so like her mother now
Wanting to know the time and place
To bring her close to her beloved.

'With all my heart I thank you now
For coming daily to my presence
It has meant so much to me
I cannot say what my heart feels
So full of radiant glow inside.'

'The purpose of my journey, Mum,
From Australia's land to Brighton here
Was to see you close at hand.
The distance and the visits now
Are tokens of my love for you.'

'I know your love and always have
I'm grateful all the same for it.
It's one to know it in my mind
Another to see, touch and feel it
With eyes and skin and cheek.'

'You are worth the visits and the trip
I'd travel to the moon and back;
Australia is like just next door
The plane comes quickly nowadays
To bring our hearts together.'

She smiled now with vast affection
Like a sunset's shimmering hues.
My heart was close to bursting now;
My frame could not contain such love
And silence spoke a lengthy kiss.

'Remember Zita Forbes, dear Mum;
"Do not yourself low estimate
World does that for you instead"
Those words for me I pass to you.'
'Yes, I'll take them for myself,' she said.

'Those words of Zita's are so true.
Did she really utter them?'
'At brink of manhood to me she said it
I remember it like yesterday'
And peace reigned in the room again.

'You'll never know your gift to me;
It passes beyond all comprehension.'
'I cannot have belief in it;
Dear Ron did so much more for you.
I was the lesser of us two.'

'It was the two of you who bore me
Two that reared me through the years.
Love of nature did Dad instil
While you a love of arts and culture
And a wider world to know.

My character's a certain blend
Of you and Dad in even balance
My life relies on both of you
I knew from depths your love of me
It stands forever in my breast.

You are united in my soul
The two are joined within my heart.
Thanks are to you both inside.
He has gone before you now
It's you I want to thank to-day.

Her leg was up upon a stool.
Flowers in the vase nearby
And wine upon the wooden table.
I looked at her and she at me
Between us was ineffable.

She smiled in light tranquillity
Looking down to childhood years
To distant Sydney where I live
And through to Argentina then
Before a time in London's centre.

But soon to Portugal she went
To become my father's happy bride.
She lived full fifty years at least
In Porto's sombre granite town
Near the ocean's mighty roar.

And birth she gave to children three
Her love for us was firm and stout
Faithful through all storms and fights
She roared for us amidst the arrows
Standing steadfast like a rock.

I went through all her family now
Jill, James, myself, Margaret and Clare
With Rupert, David and Miranda
Not leaving out our Andrew too.
She smiled in blissful happiness.

All of us your children blessed
Are happy in our lives to rest
You can be sure you've given us
A life of trusted happiness.
We thank you for it all of us.

She turned to me and said it gravely,
'Are you truly settled now?'
Twas a sombre twinkle in her eye.
'I am quite settled now at last
With Joan as wife the torture's past.

'I am so lucky with my Joan
She is a trusted wife to have.
A rare decision marrying her'
'I know I like her through and through'
'I can trust her all my life.'

'I have always liked her too
And know she can be trusted well.
It is good fortune to be wed
To one you can put trust upon.
I wish my love on both of you.'

There was a silence now of peace.
I opened up my lazer beam:
'Are you ready now to die?'
'My life's been full, I've reached the end
I'm ready now to die at last'

'You've always been so brave in life
You'll face this death with courage now.'
'I will,' she said with quiet resolve.
I held her hand to comfort her
Sadness and love dwelt in the quiet.

Then she turned and looked direct
Asking me with no deceit:
'Is there naught you have to say?'
Now was my moment to be grasped.
I'd speak direct to her at last.

'I have been a shocking bugger
In the way I've treated you
I've always loved you from the heart
Although it may look otherwise.'
'I know you have,' she simply said.

'You have done so much for me,'
What pitiable vessels are poor words.
Her answer was of generous love:
'You have done more for me you know
Than I have ever done for you.'

A silence reigned around supreme.
'I must go now, dear Mum, at last.'
I lent and kissed her on both cheeks.
Then last words she spoke to me:
'Thank you, Neville, for being you.'

I bent and kissed her twice again,
Holding hands in firmly grip.
I stood up, releasing now her hand
And walked out firmly from the room
Into the open air outside.

Of all the people I have met
She had a courage rarely met
To have her as my dearest mother
Was the rarest privilege
That fills my heart with thankfulness.

POEMS OF CHILDHOOD

All these poems call to mind my childhood. I was blessed with good fortune. I think of the many events that were so happy and full of joy. These poems though are focussed upon agony and desolation. This had its origin I believe in the fateful fact that my mother fell ill just after my birth. One of my earliest memories is of her with her leg in plaster. She developed a tubercular knee just after my birth. I was I believe affected by this event. It was pure chance that my birth coincided with this event in my mother's life. I believe that chance is a major actor in the human scene and, I believe, that psycho-analysis attributes to intentions many things which belong to chance rather than human deliberation. I think this originates from Freud's brilliant exposition in *The Psychopathology of Everyday Life*, *The Interpretations of Dreams* and *Jokes and their relation to the Unconscious*. That there are frequently intentions lying behind what seem to be chance events is certain but it has been exaggerated. What Freud says here needs to be balanced with that marvellous passage of his in *The Future of an Illusion:*

"There are the elements, which seem to mock at all human control;
the earth, which quakes and is torn apart ad buries all human life and

25

its works; water, which deluges and drowns everything in a turmoil, storms, which blow everything before them; there are diseases, which we have only recently recognized as attacks by other organisms; and finally there is the painful riddle of death, against which no medicine has yet been found, nor probably will be. With these forces nature rises up against us, majestic, cruel and inexorable; she brings to our mind once more our weakness and helplessness, which we thought to escape through the work of civilization ... Impersonal forces and destinies cannot be approached; they remain eternally remote. But if the elements have passions that rage as they do in our own souls, if death itself is not something spontaneous but the violent act of an evil Will, if everywhere in nature there are Beings around us of a kind that we know in our own society, then we can breathe freely, can feel at home in the uncanny and can deal by psychical means with our senseless anxiety."[1]

The error of attributing the Freud of *The Psychopathology of Everyday Life* to the Freud of *The Future of an Illusion* is a case of taking something which is true of a discrete domain of human experience and applying it to events that are quite outside that domain and makes a madness out of the latter. In fact it is a madness hidden within professional verbiage. Total madness is when I believe everything that happens is intentional. So what begins as a significant insight becomes, in the hands of a group addiction to the idea, a madness. There is a lust with us human beings to find a simple recipe that will explain a whole universe of phenomena. Turning chance events into deliberate intentions is how Freud understands the source of animism. This endowment of accidental happenings with an intentionality is a primitive mechanism. When I went for supervision to Wilfred Bion and told him of my patient who was late because of the snow on the ground he said to me: 'You need to tell her that God has sent that snow down to get between you and her'. Yes, even the snow, the rain or the heat has been sent by God to prevent two persons coming into communion with one another. No poet has given more potent expression to this than Andrew Marvell in his poem *The Definition of Love*. Sanity requires a recognition that many events happen to

---

[1] Freud, S. (1927). *The Future of an Illusion*. S.E. v. XXI. pp. 16–17. London: The Hogarth Press & The Institute of Psycho-Analysis.

us from chance but also that some events happen by intention. This makes an understanding of the world a more complex affair and it is this which we humans try to avoid through the implementation of a simplistic recipe. My mother's illness and disablement at the time of my birth was a chance event. Blaming her puffs me up and makes me in control of events. It puffs me up in a delusional way but diminishes the capacity of my mind. I believe that this attribution of intentionality to accidental events is a way of closing the mind into a smaller circle. This is what Freud implies in the passage quoted is that we close the actual world down into the circumference of what is familiar. We are required to expand our minds to encompass both the intentional and accidental. This expansion of mind is not just an intellectual demand but an emotional one also.

The other event that affected my early childhood was the eruption of the Second World War. I was two years old when war broke out. British subjects in Portugal, after the fall of France, were advised by the British Embassy in Lisbon to leave as it was feared that the Germans would invade Iberia. So my father prepared to go to England to join up and it was decided that my mother and her three children, together with our governess, Joan Smith, should migrate to Canada. And so it happened that when I was three we flew from Lisbon on a flying boat stopping at the Azores and Bermuda and landing in New York. We then took a train to Kingston in Canada and then went to Quebec and finally settled in Montreal where we stayed until the middle of 1943 when we returned across the Atlantic on a Portuguese liner, the Serpa Pinto. We were lucky because on its subsequent voyage it was stopped by a German submarine and British and American passengers were transported to a prison in Germany. So my parents were wrenched apart and I think this event and my mother's illness withdrew her attention from me, her youngest child. I have no doubt that she loved me as my father did also but I think her emotional attention was withdrawn from me onto her illness and the violent political events that disrupted her life. So these poems reflect, I believe, the way these events affected my own inner subjective experience.

THE ILL-CHILD

Introduction

The poetic art expresses something which cannot be expressed in prose or any other art form. This poem is concerned with my relation to my mother as a child. It has however reflections within it that come from knowledge garnered later in my life.

The Ill-Child

His face was a grinning moon
Cracking jokes in laughter
Christmas Day at Uncle John's
With cousins giggling after.

Port, wine, food and games
A theatre of sweet merriment
A microcosm of the year
Concentration of contentment.

Father and twin brother John
With hostile wives in labour
Had spawned this divers flock
Of children all in favour.

A blight upon the festival
Cracked skin about his lips
With balm Mum anointed them
His head upon her hips.

She saw the eczema of the heart
Which sorrowed into malady
In depths like Mariana's trench
Hid a foul disease in tragedy.

A picture of a floppy babe
Surprised upon the inner screen
The minute hands were stretching fast
Towards her bosom seen.

They could not reach as far as her
Lying trapped in a catatonic ilk
Consumption in her armly joints
A reckless draught of unboiled milk

The raucous fun and cheerfulness
Was blended to a dark addiction
Of sombre crime that poisoned it
The milk submitting to corruption.

This arcane knowledge in her soul
Brought torture into Birth's birthday
What should have been a day of joy
Was darkened by guilt's painful ray.

Legacy of cruel past
Blackening her motherhood
Transferred womblike
Into her darling's babyhood.

What betrayed to him her secret woe
Was his mouth's cracked skin
A wedding bathed in sparkling wine
Disguised the secret sin.

Outer mirth was an imposture
Through a signature in sin
That left an imprint on her mind
Which ugly lips reproached her in.

Dear Ron was kind and courteous
One of heaven's innocents
His eyes stone blind
To passions of a darker sense.

Her love was of a double kind
A woman's breasts and eyes
Had intertwined with hers
In Argentina's Buenos Aires.

This passion hired her heart
Intermittently in memory's house
No love could ever measure it
Troubling now her marriage vows.

This darling boy she loved
Lived in her hidden secret
The Baptist was reproaching her
For unfaithfulness unmet

The cracked white skin
Shone bright with Tabor's light
Shrivelling his mind to ashes
Begetting a sadist god in powerful might.

The gold-haired boy was hidden now
Like flesh inside a porcupine
With quills of burning rage
Against his mother's natural sign.

Snarling at unrighteousness
And rooting out injustices
It was a perfect tailor's fit
For sacerdotal vertices.

He savaged London's streets
With violent hateful gospelling
Father in the snake-pit now
From sinner's den he'd mother bring.

He blamed the sin upon convention
Beloved by father's piety
Poor mother was its precious victim
Her sin its new satiety.

A dry-skinned priest he was
Growling at polite tradition
Surrounded left by worshippers
And right by opposition.

He raced with fury round his parish
Making converts to his vision
With fierce devotion to the truth
Of the devil's own possession.

A broken congregation
To God a most repulsive sight
Was only broken skin
In mother's darkened might.

BUTTERFLY BOY

Introduction

This poem encircles my immediate family, the wider family with its circle of cousins, the pursuit of butterflies, condemnation, public school and alienation. It weaves a theme between the earlier and the later. It encompasses a wider family scene than Ill Child.

Butterfly Boy

He was enwrapped entire
By a trance of absolute love.
The kindly face of Uncle Maurice
Smiled sweetly now in his direction.
That love in Maurice dwelt in all
His uncle's, aunts and cousins too.

It was as sure as firmament
As certain as the stars above
And solid as the earth beneath
Only a meteor as large as earth
Could shatter and fragment
Its hugely cast-iron frame.

They loved us all this family
In days and months and years as well
It never was a passing whim
Or sudden burst of shooting star.
It was as lasting as the seasons
And firm as God in Heaven.

Nothing could ever break this Eden
It was rooted like the English yew
In the very loamiest soil;
Recorded in the Doomsday book,
It now stands firm beside the Thames
At Ankerwycke, near Runnymede.

That yew was darkest hidden
Amidst cavernous horrid trees
With slime and cantankerous weeds
Surrounding its huge diameter
In its shadow did poor Harold fall
Victim to the French dictator.

This was no river loved by Maurice
But the mustard muddy Douro
In the heights of Portugal
Swirling languid through ravines
Washing past the family vines
And on to Porto's lodges.

He gave this boy a camera
A present for his birthday
On reaching to the age of ten.
It was not just a casual gift
But something considered lengthily
With tenderest care and love.

The boy felt love embracing him
Massaging shoulders, cheeks and legs.
His very being was bathed in it.
This other-Eden, demi Paradise
An idyll world begot for him
By Ron and Norah's loving union.

'See that Rock on mountain's edge',
Said Maurice pointing to a Ridge
Placed between two mountain tops.
'Even on the hottest day
A cool breeze blows upon its face
And rewards the journey to the top.

'It is a place beloved at times
By the Pasha butterfly.
They like the cool breeze in shade;
It is a hot and tiring climb
But almost sure you are to find
The Pasha in most gracious flight.'

The boy he had a fine collection
Of lepidoptera of Iberian kind.
Yet the Pasha still eluded him.
Father and son had mourned together
This absence among fine specimens
Resigned themselves to imperfection.

Maurice's words aroused a spark
That soon became a forest fire
His breast was flaming with desire.
He would the Maurice mountain climb
And catch the Pasha butterfly
Surprise and triumph over father.

So out he crept one early morn
Armed with net and killing-bottle.
Adults all were still asleep
In the complacent Indian bungalow
On the slopes of hither Pinhão
Where Bomfim nestled amid the schist.

Up the ochre vine-clad path
Towards wrought-iron gates
That severed Eden from alien mobs
Passing quick through second gate
That brought him back within the frame
Of a loving family's embrace.

The quinta like Siddhartha's palace
Protected him from heart's writhing
Through meeting age, death and suffering.
Channa's ride outside those gates
Stirred passion's tyrant guarding him
Against the pain of love's embrace.

His pace was quick and fearful now
His tremulous heart missed a beat.
How many doctors had heard that heart
Through stethoscopes and nodding heads
Declared the boy an invalid
To mother's fearful ears at least.

The heart is such a fear-filled organ
Like engine in an aeroplane
It putts away through night and day
And all of life depends on it.
Most people never think on it.
It's just within like sun and rain.

But injected into this boy's mind
Was a constant fear of death.
This dark guardian never left him.
When the heart did miss a beat
Or overcome with breathlessness
Death's shadow now emcompassed him.

It drove him out from family's love
Into the jaw's of Calvin's church.
They all were Catholics so devout
To Sunday Mass they went each week
And every month they shrove themselves
And to the Sacrament they always went.

The boy went too with full devotion
To Church, prayers and Communion too
From without he looked the same
Chanting hymns, reciting prayers
As mother, father, sister and brother
And uncles, aunts and cousins too.

But hidden in those Roman rites
A Protesting heart was beating.
It rumbled 'gainst hypocrisy
And hated Rome's complacency
It was a spark now buried deep
But destined to become a blaze.

It was hidden from his view
Just like that brooding Doomsday yew
All he knew was determined passion
To reach the rock that Maurice knew
And catch securely in his net
The two-tailed Pasha butterfly.

On he went in early morn
Up the curving golden path
Of Douro landscape to the farm.
The sun was up, the sky was blue
Only a dark patch of cloud
Between hills over to the west.

The boy he turned and noticed it
But flicked his head in dire contempt
Naught would stop his heart's intent
Of reaching to the Maurice mount
To catch inside his awful net
The beautiful Pasha butterfly.

From sunny schist to blackened valley
Down he travelled into it
Selecting up a cork-screw path
Amidst gum-cystus undergrowth
Where speckled woods and skippers too
Ingested nectar's nurturing.

Like babies sucking at the breast
And making milk so warm within
The province of the common herd
This temple guardian despised
And kept his precincts all pure
For religion's brutal elite.

His net was not for such as these
The collection had its fill of them
He passed them by disdainfully
Pushing through the undergrowth
Ignoring scratches to the skin
And fog-horn blaring within.

Nothing daunted him at all
Even shadow from the cloud
Shutting out the sunlight now
Only made him more determined.
No cautious word or friend's advice
Could touch inside the inner ear.

He it was inside the net
In a monstrous ogre's clasp
A clammy hand enclosed the heart
That drove an icicle within
And nearly stopped that precious pump
Freezing blood stone cold

Cast down yourself I'll hold you up
Preventing you from injury.
'Do it, do not be afraid,'
Spoke the Enemy within
Those ancient feet in Douro now
Took possession of his breast.

He was now a shrine divine
Treading footprints of the saints
Flagellation of the body
Contemptuous of indulging flesh
Removing him from family pleasure
Port and stilton banned forever.

His dearest father, glass in hand
Sniffing expertly dark colour
And noticing a false aroma
That would destroy a precious blend
But unrefined in sophist culture
To give to it linguistic nurture.

His courtesy was rare indeed
He loved his boy with troubled heart
His daughter made him tremble too.
Only his other son did tread
A normal path in family rites
Not taking him to alien sights.

Who was this wife that he had wed?
From low in southern hemisphere.
What enigmatic puzzle rose in her
To blight the purest family blood?
With strangest perils in Troy's walls
Family's castle was in danger now.

He withdrew in fear within the keep
Behind the mightiest portcullis.
None could penetrate within
Except the Father Confessor
And even he caught just a glimpse
Of a tyrant's savage madness.

A mighty bomb behind those walls
Was guarded by taught visages
And blind devotion to the Church
Not weekly now to Mass he went
But every day in fierce intent
Pouring prayer to a greedy God.

This bomb-seed planted within
Was hidden from his intimates
But captured hit the boy's gentleness
And burned a panic in the heart
The fires of Hell licked into him
Replacing love with awesome fear.

The family love could not reach him
The rock of Maurice darkened now
A storm cloud full enveloped it.
The boy was clutching onto it
The Church Rock now to rescue him
From Hell's eternal fires within

The rain it pelted down on him
And turned to icy hail inside
Remembering cold Ampleforth
Stone corridors in early morn
To chapel's gloomy rituals
The only gate to Heaven now.

Those borstals for the upper class
To make scamps into gentlemen
Young boys to them are billeted
And in this foundry are melted down
The quaint, the charm and oddity
Into grey amorphous blocks.

To this concentration camp
They sent the boy for education
To make him fit for commerce class.
Unhappiness reached vast proportion
He thought it was a penitence
For a sacrilege of youth.

The family gathered for Communion
At Holy Mass on Christmas Day.
With shriven souls and bodies fasted
They knelt at Communion rail
The organ played its sonorous tones
God smiling on his loyal ones.

The boy had broken holy fast
With chocolate in the early morn.
Communion was forbidden him
For breaking this most solemn rule
'Twas too late with ciborium near
In worldly fear he took the host.

He was now in mortal sin
His spirit black as Hitler's soul
He belonged within to Satan's pack
The abyss between Dad's smiling face
And the state of inner soul
Was sealed impassable.

He could shrive his soul-slate clean
And start New Year in purity.
The friendly priest smiled warmly.
'Bless me, Father, for I've sinned'
But confess the crime he didn't dare
The hand of Satan closed in again.

Not now one sacrilege but two
Macbeth-like was his gathering soul.
Instead of nurturing young soul
Each sacrament did torture it
And place him deeper into Hell
Death would come and put him there.

The devils danced around him now
He was in their power for sure
The Douro's earthy sunlight dimmed
Estranged he was from homely warmth
An alien in this happy fold
Their laughing voices all outside.

Outer ritual of benign communion
With his other family members
Was a sunny mask disguising
A dark cloudy soul within
Cutting his psyche into two
Making him all broken too.

The hail was lashing at the stone
A gale thundered into him.
He gripped the Rock and held it tight
It was his only safety now
He was fluttering inside the net
The killing-bottle mocking him.

As storm-clouds shatter little planes
This lalique crystal so delicate
Broken in a thousand bits
Reflecting each with rapier lights
That entered to his broken brain
And made an utter mess of it.

Six years he spent at holy college
His body draped in flowing cassock
He was ordained a massing priest
Rome's God and Cardinal smiled on him
Family kneeling for priest's new blessing
Even the boy believed in it.

The shattered glass looked whole again
With veneration all around
Heads bowed again in *hyperdulia*
A sense of tingling touched his skin
And drew him far from broken bits
That his insides were mostly made of.

The family woke midst thunder storm.
Where was their gentle fair haired boy?
The vineyard workers were sent in search
Scouring hills in deluge flood
Father saw the net had gone
And guessed his boy's expedition.

They found him limp nearby the Rock.
His body broken 'cross its lap
Mother's heart was desolate
She took the body, crying on it
Gazing sadly at the net
Lying all muddy, torn and wet.
* * * *

Wherefrom this human arsenic?
That took him from sunlit warmth
To sludge-like desperation?
What was its fearful origin?
That wrested him from family love
Casting him to darkest hell?

This curled-cobra lying in his heart
Was summoned in for restoration
Of injury incurred when sucking
At his mother's fulsome bosom
Her loving eyes joined to his
When suddenly they glued upon his twin

Leaving him in outer darkness
A vacuum of the heart
No picture could be drawn of it
Or spoken or described
A black Nazi serpent was embraced
To represent the nothingness.

Why was its power so great?
Overthrowing the family warmth?
It was to make the mother look
To bring maternal glance to him
Unnoticed was this tiny lapse
That was immense for him inside.

No speech could make the people hear
A Catholic sacrament was needed
Joining words and actions
With a new-found super-glue
To bring bowed heads to recognition
In hearts and well as heads.

Mother cupped the corpse upon her lap
Desolate tears flooded immobility
The life was gone only deadness there
She became a marble statue
It stands upon the hilltop now
For passers-by to point it to visitors.

CARMEN

Introduction

I was brought up in Oporto in the north of Portugal. When I go down the Avenida da Boavista which stretches from the sea towards the city with its elegant poplars I feel a thump of nostalgia. I have always loved Monet's *Poplars on the Epte*. I suspect that those beautiful paintings remind me of the poplars on the Boavista.

María was the commonest name for a woman in Portugal. Two of our three maids were called María do Carmo so we called one María and the other Carmen. María had been a maid to my father for ten years before he married. So she started service with him in 1922. When my father married in 1932 she became maid to my mother and father and then to the whole family as one child after another was born. She was our cook.

Carmen came to us when I was six, on our return from Canada. She was severe but loved us all and held us always within her disciplined guardianship. She was a second mother to me and I loved her. It was a love founded on respect.

I visited her when she was old in a retirement home in the centre of Oporto. She spoke the simple sentence: *Gosto de viver; tenho pena*

45

de morrer (I like living; I am sorry that I have to die). She had been with us as our maid for fifty-five years. I felt that telling me that she liked living was also a generous gift to me: telling me that living in our family had been a joy. I took with me to visit her our two boys. I told her that she was my *segunda mãe* (second mother) and she thanked me for saying it. It was so clear that she was loved by the other women in the home. She cared for them with a gentle concern. As I left she said to me 'I don't think I will see you again' and I was sad. Six months later she died.

Carmen

She was there ever caring
Standing watchful guarding
I was no latchkey child
No empty house was mine
Carmen made it home.

I fear an empty house
Falling into empty void
A scream brought Carmen to my side
Always guarding, caring
I belonged to her I knew.

She cared for me as mother
As if I were born of her
She our servant, we her babies
When we ate she stood watching
Always guarding, caring.

Without her I cannot care for me
I was lost without her in prep school
'You cannot even make a bed',
The harsh headmaster said.
I cried for Carmen's caring.

Far from Carmen on cold Yorkshire moor
Her care-ful face was out of sight.
Long lonely empty corridors
Peopled with walking corpses
I was a corpse myself.

I sinned against the family canons
Was banished from their hearth
Carmen knew a deeper me
'Far better be a married man
Than a bitter-living priest'
Her simplicity saw deep.

Not deceived by outer rites
'I love living' she said
She knew what living meant
It is a movement of the heart
A ripple in the depths.

What no family member knew
She passed proudly on to me
All my life I treasure it
I thank her now for giving it
She might have kept it in.

Her simple words before she died:
'I love living and wish not to die'
Those generous words she passed to me
Quickly dying thereafter
Bequeathing rich words for my inheritance

She was rich within
Living among companions warm
They loved her all
As she cared and prayed for them
So she loved living.

My natural mother
Was rich in stirling worth
But desolate in inner spirit
Living was a sour spirit
In a rich retirement home.

Carmen was living in the poor house
In tatty living quarters
Close to warm presences
She did not want to die
She loved living.

She was always there guarding caring
I was no latchkey child
The home she made is in my mind
Tradition's homely hearth
Guarding me against modern emptiness.

FR. KENNETH

Introduction

I have a gentle memory for this quiet tender-hearted monk who poured a healing balm into my soul when I was at the Junior House at Ampleforth. I was at St. Martin's School for four terms from eleven to thirteen. Unlike most English Public Schools, Ampleforth had a Junior House where boys stayed for two years from twelve to fourteen before moving into the Upper School. It was while I was in the Junior House that the event happened that is recorded in this poem. I must therefore have been about thirteen at the time.

Fourteen years later when I was a priest on the parish hearing many confessions of people, especially Irish men and women, who were tortured by guilt about sexual thoughts and feelings I tried to be towards them as Fr. Kenneth had been towards me.

Father Kenneth

He was a quiet gentle man.
Looking kindly at the fair-haired boy.
Kneeling fearfully to shrive himself.
His knees cushioned beside the priest.

He had sinned a mortal sin.
A sword, cutting his holy bond to God.
His soul was devoured by devils
In the very depths of hell.

"I've sinned a very grievous sin,"
He whispered to the priest.
"Tell me what it is, dear boy,
Our loving Jesus will forgive."

The boy he sobbed and wet his cheek
His throat was choking, he could not speak.
Fr. Kenneth stretched out his hand
Touching his shoulder tenderly.

What had this fair child done?
To anger God so heinously?
He'd consumed the Sacred Host
Breaking the sacred midnight fast.

It was on Easter morning
Greeted by father's plaintive smile
"We'll go all together to the sacrament
As a family gift to God."

The boy returned his smile
Seeing pleasure in his father's face.
Then memory of a fudgy chocolate
Swam before his inner eyes.

He struggled helpless 'twixt God and father,
Displease his earthly Dad or the eternal God?
Father's expectant smile he could not betray
Better to hurt his distant God.

He'd go after to confess his sin
It would soon be wiped away
His father's fragile pleasure
Would remain intact to-day.

So to the altar rail he went
Beside his mother, sister and brother
Father smiling happily at his
Newly god-born brood.

He put out his tongue
Like a nestling to its mother
The priest placed upon it
The Body and Blood of Jesus Christ.

The devils cackled in obscene laughter
He may look a fair-haired child of God
But now he belongs to us
His soul is branded with our sign.

Outside the church was sunny light
The family walking home in it.
The boy was holding mother's hand
His soul was writhing hopelessly.

Next day he walked alone to Church
It was a drizzling wettish day
He saw the cassocked priest
Enter the wood confessional

The boy he knelt in coffin darkness
'What sins have you committed?'
He heard a savage angry God
Chiding him his fearful sin.

He hid in terror from the priest
'I forgot my prayers and told a lie'
Murmured the frightened boy
A Latin pardon sentenced him.

He'd added now a further sin
A sacrilege to keep it in
And mock God's mercy
In the dark confessional.

So he went from sin to sin.
Every time he received the host
He was drinking of the devil's cup
God's light was distant from his soul.

More deeply was he placed in hell
Each month and year of Catholic practice
Placed him further into Satan's clutches
Death would seal him into deepest Hell.

Then gentle Fr. Kenneth touched his head
'No need to tell; you are forgiven'
The fair haired boy looked at his face
Confessing to him everything.

'Ego te absolvo in nomine Patris et Filii
et Spiritui Sancti - you are forgiven now.
God loves you, my child, go hither
In love and cheerfulness.'

QUICKSAND

Introduction

This poem records a moment that happened when I was aged fifteen. At that moment I put all my trust in God. Only later did I come to realize that this God in whom I trusted was an idol. I had not listened in my heart to the prophet Isaiah:

> "They are ignorant, those who carry about
> their idol of wood,
> those who pray to a god
> that cannot save." Ch. 45. v. 20.

And I worshipped an idol, in different forms, for fifty years.

Quicksand

On a mundane Sunday beach
Covered with light ocre sand
Which stretched beyond my reach
I was left only with God's wrath.

Like a puny Harlow monkey
I clung to it most desperately
All vanished 'cept this phantom God
Ingested in immediately.

It was not a companion presence
That granted me some quiet solace
But a merciless tyrant-Nazi god
The worst virus in the human race.

Yet it saved me in the quicksand
Pretending to be a solid stone
Attached to the planet's firmament
I did not know I was alone.

All solids round me liquified
Home faces razed to desolation
All but this exacting god
Demanding me in isolation.

I preached to vacant stares
My proud new invention
More real it was to me
Than tales of lying sensation.

Two teenagers vied within
A fourteen and eighteen year old
The first was a visionary
The second a crazy impulse bold.

The vision needed company
To share and understand
But in the midst of the devout
There was none to take my hand.

ST. MARTIN'S

Introduction

There is a theme in these poems of being cast out of the hearth of love and warmth. This poem is chronologically the first boyhood experience of this at the age of eleven. I went to a prep school for four terms at St. Martin's School which, at that time, was housed in Kirkdale Manor in the little village of Nawton in the North Riding of Yorkshire. St. Martin's Day which fell on 11th November was celebrated always with a large bonfire.

Bonfire at St. Martin's

Sister and Brother were schooled in England now
Nevilinho stayed with Mum and Dad
"I'll be treated as a child no more;
You treat me as a babe which makes me sore."
Father surrendered to this *teimoso* lad.

As the car drew up to Kirkdale Manor
Casting Babe upon this gloomy Moor
Babe inside was withering
As he watched the car now vanishing
Down the drive it went and left him poor.

He turned into the grim-walled mansion
To heedless boys in their hurried race
Caring naught for this new arrival
Rushing past him in battling thrall.
'It's this way,' said a freckly kindly face.

He knelt, asking God to care for him.
A skinny mantle covering his shoulders
The chapel was his Sunday home
Where to Porto now, his mind could roam
All days were huge mountain boulders

A bonfire burned on Armistice Day
St. Martin's Day of recollection
The flames lit up the cold dark night
While shivering boys watched the sight
Burnt in it was small babe's affection.

His face became a dried up chip
His skin-flake lips he really hated
In asthmatic strangle was his breathing
Bronchiole tubes with gunge were seathing
His body ash-like had been cremated

Like a felled sapling on the ground
Its leaves all curled and dried
A shadow of this happy male
Victim to this darkened gaol
At Martinmas he cried inside.

He could not make his bed aright
Hospital corners he could not enjoy
Fifteen tiny points he earned
The perfect thirty he never learned
Of his dormitory he was the shame-boy

Granny knots at cubs he made
He could not tie his laces right
In sport a gangling asthmatic lad
His hanging shirt made him look bad
Fly buttons never fastened tight.

He fumbled through the routine day
At him headmaster hurls abuse
His shouts becoming panic-seeds
Numbing his own direst needs
He felt inside he was no use

A mess inside and outside too
The doctors ordered pills and cream
They placed the boy in isolation
A heart murmur was their declaration
He was the laughing-stock of all his team.

Such was the Bonfire at St. Martins
The heart shrivelling from cinders burning
Changing in this prison camp
A happy smiling scamp
Into sad wiseness too early turning.

CLINICAL POEMS

Some poems have been inspired by incidents in the consulting-room—either thoughts I have had or thoughts that a patient has given voice to. I record them here. There is desperation in them all. They capture for me the fear and desolation that crowd daily into my consulting-room.

The Bear cub

My mother left me up a tree
And walked away for ever
The horizon was an empty space
And friendless light bore into me.

Leering faces shot my heart
Night is massed with demon terrors
Naught can ever calm me now
Or drive the fears away.

Time has no meaning now
Empty time is all there is
The days of week are empty slots
With colours dancing in and out.

Five weeks, a day or just an hour
Is jammed or broadened to infinity
A mother's absence is timelessness
And days and hours are all the same.

Buried alive

It felt a relief
As I sank down within
The warm soft earth.

Then a fear gripped tight
I can't get out.
They've lowered a pipe
Into my mouth.

Water and air
Cools my fright.
Then a bullet smashes
Down the pipe to my mouth.

My tongue is all blood
And my teeth are in bits
I want to get out
That's my deepest desire

But they cannot believe
With my teeth smashed up
And my tongue pouring blood.
My words are transmuted
To their opposite sense.

I lie there in panic
Giving up the attempt.
I hate death now
As it grins in the tunnel.

Dances with wolves

The wolf knows how to hunt
He's done it all his life.
The man offers food
With outstretched arm.

It's a danger to be at his mercy
Although the food is so easy
Coming doglike every day
But I fear the look in his eye

The man offers his finger
To touch me like God to Adam
But what a mess he made
Of the human world entire

Is this one of his specimens
Right out here in the prairie
Why didn't he stay in his niche
In ancient Olduvai Gorge?

I know my skills as a hunter
The prairie is my world.
I won't be tempted to easy life
In the arms of treacherous man.

I prefer the savage wilds
My nose and teeth I trust better
And a lot of hunger too
Than the crafty wiles of man

Fish in a shoal

A wave comes from the left
And that's the way I move,
My tail is a rudder
But currents are a pilot
That decide every heading.

The currents are a pressure
That I'm unable to resist
My tail can only move me
Quicker down their channels
I am their helpless victim.

A tone of voice; a raised eyebrow
A haughty manner or nose in the air,
A suspicious look or a rude gaze
These are the currents that drive me
Along life's waterways.

I'm in a shoal with others,
I feel their bodies swish
And I swirl with them all;
They are the current of my life
And there's no soul to resist.

Trust and thought

Flesh to flesh - that's all I know
Absence send me into madness.
My hair falls out; my teeth break
My mind starts swimming dizzily round
And I fall into a vacuum of swirling emptiness

Space is filled with demons
With Goya's leering faces;
They look with malevolent eyes
And I rush away from their gaze.
There's no good figure in all their crowd.

I rush and flee - from where I don't know
And no one ever stops me,
No friend in this frenzy dares show a face.
The awful hobgoblins pulling me round
There's no one to halt me at all.

In this world no trust exists
The swirling horror is there instead.
No place for trust so no thought either.
Thought is born from trust
And trust is absence held.

Oh where is that presence
That's all I want.
It can't be named
When it's there there is trust
But without it black madness.

Two castles

Can you see those birds in flight?
Or the duck the eagle's chasing?
See the cloud cell vanished in rain
As empty as if it'd never been there.
Can you see, can you see from your castle over there?

There's a star can't you see
I can't - there's a cloud in the way
All hope is gone
I'll seal up my castle
Oh, look now - another star - look
I can see I can see

It's slow without a telephone
Only stars and clouds and sun
And sky and rain and thunder
I can only point
I have no speech
My language are the elements.

ADULT POEMS

IN-GRATITUDE is an adult poem but it stands on its own as it is so crucially important and stretches from childhood, to adulthood and through to the end of life.

There are a few other poems which I have been moved to write and I am ashamed at the poems which I have *not* written. There have been so many moments of emotional significance which cried out for a poem and they have remained unrealized. This is my own loss. An artistic expression always enriches ones life, it expands experience and makes it more fruitful. So these are a few scatterings among the possible many.

BECOMING GOD AND HALLUCINATION
AT HENDON AERONAUTICAL MUSEUM

Introduction

What is the nature of my existence? What is the nature of existence as a whole? How on earth did I become a conscious being and how did mankind emerge on this planet? These existential questions have been with me since childhood. I remember when I was an eight year old in a house in Miramar, a little village south of Oporto, which my parents rented together with Reg and Auriel Cobb. I remember asking Reg questions like 'Why do the stars only shine at night, Uncle Reg?' and 'How do fish breathe?' and 'Why was Jesus born in Palestine instead of Portugal?' On and on I went till at breakfast one day Uncle Reg said, in an irritated tone, 'Will you please stop asking questions?' I cannot remember whether I stopped pestering him but I am glad to say that his admonition did not stop me going on asking questions and I have continued this way all my life. It is for this reason that I have always been attracted to the existential philosophers and, more recently, particularly the writings of Paul Tillich. Both these poems have that existential theme.

Becoming god

On a pinnacle of light
In the midst of darkness
It's not in place or time
In it I am and me in it
Twas there I became.

It was clear as a bell
Sounding in the dawn
As frightening as frozen life
Standing as beacon
For the mind to become.

It happened in God
Or God became man.
To be humble then
Is life's awe filled task.

Hallucination at Hendon Aeronautical Museum

Staring at a flying machine,
Hanging from a high white ceiling
By threadlike nylon wires.
I was looking at his side
Planelike from a window wide.

He was walking solidly
Alone upon an open floor
Looking at these fragile flyers
Resting quiet from turbulence.
In this morgue-like ambience.

It was man that caught my eye
How had his being come to be?
Not only in this plane museum
But walking on the earth at all
A thought that gut-like did appal.

Geological time was telescoped
Yesterday he was a chimp
The day before a vervet monkey
A week before a crocodile
A month ago a fish'n the Nile.

Focussed in this lonesome plodder
Walking in casual concentration
Upon museum's spacious floor
Embodying the human race
In unity of time and place.

Was this suited substance
What language called a man?
Or was I in some vast delusion?
How had his being come to be
What was it that eluded me?

A fact taken all for granted
Became the huge-est question mark
Burrowing into life's foundations
With it all projects were suffused
And made my past all confused.

Beside a canal in Worcestershire
A frog jumped from beneath my feet
I looked at it with tenderness;
From its genes I am descended
In that sight something was mended.

The frame that silhouetted 'man'
Dissolved and made me humble now
Making cousinhood with fish and bird
With amphibians and reptiles too
All the denizens of the zoo.

The lens through which I viewed him now
Was latent in my mind before
But trained upon the world without:
The starry heavens and evolution
From which I looked without devotion.

My being was within him now
I was not looking from without
For him and I were oned together
This compound now has changed the lens
Making what was past the present tense.

'A change of focus?'
Chimes the sophomore.
'You are outside as I once was
No exegesis can enlighten you
For you live within a different hue'

'There are many ways of being a man'
Wrote our ancient E.M. Forster.
My own has at last been found.
My being has veered to its own direction
Which is to ask life's basic question.

FIRST BORN

Introduction

Surely one of the most important moments in a man's life is when a child is born to him? It was so vivid an experience that I wrote this poem in a shabby café in Shepherd's Bush an hour or so after the birth. I wrote it then as it appears now. I don't think I have changed it since writing it about midday on 5th October 1975.

The first born

The quiet voice that tells
Of birth by Caesar's section
There is no time to fear it
Or manage comprehension

The mother lay there silent
Cheated of her labour
But how could she resent it
When it comes as infant's saviour?

For labour to a woman
Is proof of womanhood
The surgeon's rustling haste
Forgets what no mother could.

The father sits alone
Imagining blood and hustle
And knowing that his dear one
Lies oblivious of all the bustle.

The nurse appears and says
'Do you want to see your son?'
He looks at the screwed up face
And barely believes it's come

The mother comes around
And the little baby sees,
The expression on her face
No lines on earth could seize.

He's growing tough and strong
No need to fear he's weak.
It's Mum and Dad who will be frail
When he is at his peak.

BLACK POPLAR

Introduction

When we lived at No. 27 Daleham Gardens we had a beautiful black poplar in the garden. It was huge and the wind rustled its leaves in a way that is characteristic of poplar trees. It was while we were living there in contented complacency that we decided to leave London and move to Australia. This poem charts that change.

Black poplar

As the wind blew, the tree turned to spirit
Clacking the leaves like a soft castanet.
As he lay a'bed listening with ears all intent
Upon Daleham's orchestral instrument
God's stare prodding a soft mind-set.

No other tree gave a note like this
With however much skill the wind blew.
Only the leaves of a poplar so high
Rattled a note so much like a sigh
Making its singular note to him true.

It rose from the ground, a volcanic eruption
Its trunk as thick as a Roman rampart.
Not as those elegant ones in France
Poplars on the Epte in a fairy dance
Its quavering foliage broke him apart.

Its leaves oddly joined to the stalk
A Stradivarius crafted by artful nature
The note of a baby's rattle he heard
As he lay in the bed it seemed so absurd
To be lifted down to a childlike stature.

It lowered him into a frightening font
A life is beginning all over again
At least a score of years away
But telescoped now just into to-day
Heaven scouts thoughts of miserly train.

It was achievement's time of complacency
Society does powerfully flatter and praise:
'You're father of a respectable household
An admired wife and two sons we behold',
'So I'll stay as I am to the end of my days.'

Into this silvery pond of still water
A stone of disquiet plunged in
The self-satisfied mask fitted tight
But the stomach-soul squirmed in the night
Wary hounds were now baying within.

The branches were noisily heaving
Leaves fluttering in the autumn air
An inner murmur was plaintively calling
To challenge the world and stop stalling.
Fast chasing the ostrich out of his lair.

He was deeply buried in an open grave
Guarded by the castle's watchful sentry
Marvellous Science the wind cannot tame
Despite moonrockets and much of the same
The invader is whining for immediate entry.

The most hidden place is transparent
Clearly visible to everyone's eyes
When the sunlight is savagely bright
It blinds even the very best sight
People of each sex, age and size.

The sighing breath through the leaves of the poplar
Its rustling stirs the deep sleeping spirit,
Aroused by the sound of the chattering wind
It is freeing a soul that had silently sinned,
Fanning the flame of a flickering inwit.

So now God's breath entered his hearth
Blowing his thoughts out of Hampstead
Flinging them around the globe's surface
Circling the world with the tightest embrace
Until planting themselves in a new southern homestead.

THE NEWSPAPER SELLER

Introduction

I was buying a newspaper on a street corner in San Francisco. She looked at me and saw the 'dilly-bag' which I always carry slung around my shoulders. Her concern for me and her romantic love on Sydney took me into my mother's arms and her tender love for me.

The newspaper seller

Tartish Lips
Implanted on a
Blank White Face
Spoke of wistful loss

By plane to Sydney
From San Francisco
Is far above my means
Its on another planet.

Her eyes my mother were
Gently resting on my face
The worry buried deep
On the surface now it came

Protect that bag from maddies
This is a nasty town.
Return in haste to Sydney
That is my favourite town.

She saw her wayward son
Kissing with her looks
Enfolding precious baby
In warm thin arms.

POETRY SPORE

Introduction

I had written many of the poems here recorded but did not value them. Then I started attending a poetry seminar, chaired by Jane Adamson. She led me to realize that a poem contains a thought but one that can only be captured through the poetic art.

Thinking is not confined within the circumference of Science, not within the perimeter of Philosophy, not within the halls of Academia. We have to go outside all this to catch the deepest thoughts, the ones that change the emotional climate of a whole age or culture.

So this poem charts a debt of gratitude to Jane Adamson. I don't think this book would exist unless she had awakened the spore. At the time of writing this I had also been reading Dubos's biography of Pasteur.

The spore of poetry

Pass along quiet landscape
Toil in earthquake's testament,
Volcano's searing lava too
Or battle-bombed old tenement.

Pasteur knows that here
In a such unlikely mound
Rest bacillus spores of poesy
Cocooned within the ground.

For sixty years they hid there
In his childhood fancying
His volcanic blight of youth
And professional somersaulting.

Then came Jane the Baptist
Armed with silent art
That waked the spores to life
Inside his conscious part.

Spores lay still for many years
They spring to life when gently meet
A human being's atmosphere
With precision-timing heat.

Jane's no dupe to propaganda
Or fashion's fluctuation
But passes on so generously
Her soul's own intuition.

This it is that breathes new life
Upon the trance-like spore
That lay within for 60 years
'Til Jane did pass before.

DOG'S PASSING

Introduction

There are certain crude divisions into which it is possible to divide the human race: those who love opera and those who don't, those who love reading and those who don't, those who love dogs and those who don't. I am one of those who loves dogs. I never pass a dog on the street without giving it a loving and nostalgic glance. I was brought up with dogs and when I don't have one there is an ache at the centre of my being.

After arriving in Australia we acquired a labrador puppy and called her Jeannie and she lived with us for thirteen years until she died. This poem was written after her death.

Jeannie's passing

I cannot do else but die,
I know you love me tenderly,
I'd love to kiss you all some more
I'd travel with you if I could
But body-life has ebbed away.

Nature's decree I cannot flout
'A dozen years is your ration'
I know not why it is so short
My cousin elephant and you
Have many times my briefly coil.

Remember though my years of yore
I raced you all along the beach
Madly twirling back and forth
Seven times your energy
Was packed within my thirteen years.

'We walked a mile' I heard you say
For every mile I raced seven.
Honour's reply to that decree:
I'll pack my time a sevenfold
With ecstasy of full time living.

Remember me you always will
My swimming with you in the pool
My wagging tail at every greeting
The smile upon my happy face.
My life's imprinted on your hearts,
My serviced body rests in quiet.

'ATHEIST'S GOD'

Introduction

In my late teens and early twenties I read with a devouring zeal the works of G.K. Chesterton. Then Sin entered my soul and I left that early love of mine and I was waylaid by that perverse spirit, known as fashion. To be respected in the modern world I had to don the cloak of Marx, of Freud, of Sartre. Then I would be an esteemed figure in the contemporary secular world.

But slowly a 'still small voice' beckoned me back to my first love and I re-read Chesterton. First I read his biography of Bernard Shaw, then his biography of Francis of Assisi, then his biography of Thomas Aquinas and then his great classics *Heretics* and *Orthodoxy*. In the latter book I came across a fantastic passage which I decided to turn into a poem. The poem does not do justice to his prose but I hope it might tempt the reader to go and read *Orthodoxy* and come to the passage on which this poem is based.

Chesterton had a quality that I have never met in such natural undiluted form in any other person or writer. He disagreed powerfully with many of his contemporaries and the 'negative spirit' in the 'moderns', as he called them, but his boundless joy for the authors whose mental philosophies he so vigorously opposed is amazing. He loved Shaw, he loved H.G. Wells, he loved Rudyard Kipling but their attitude to life he abhorred but all these contemporaries of his loved him. They knew in their hearts that it was a joyous love that animated his heart, although he believed that all these men were not just wrong but severely wrong.

So, after a long betrayal, I have come back to Chesterton, my first love.

The atheist's god

Those bowing to God in each age
Singing with gusto to Goodness
Offering hymns of glory to Greatness
Adoring his loving tenderness
GKC alone dared to add courage

Courage goes to life's breaking point
Going way beyond the break
Doing it for galaxy's sake
Knowing to-morrow's world is at stake
Mankind's future it will anoint.

Man may live in a timeless torture
His soul stretched to its tightest
His spirit remains at its brightest
His courage at its very highest
Making of death a fearless adventure

I approach a matter so dire and profound
Fearing my phrases fall down all wrong
For a more skilful expression I long
For with saints and the holy I do not belong
They dared not tread on so holy a ground.

In that shattering tale of the Passion
The author of all in a manner undreamt
Something agnostics and atheists cannot attempt
Holding the infinite in abject contempt
Believing agony's doubt to be not in fashion.

Tempting belongs to God not to us many
God tempts man, his own mettle to test
He knows for each what is best
Squeezing goodness from a deep down chest
God tempted God in Gethsemane

Satan tempted man with a lie
God tempted God with a doubt
Deep darkness encircled him all about
When the world shook and thundered a shout
And the sun was wiped from the sky

It was not the pain that nails did waken
His gentle hands endured the pain
The Crown of Thorns he could disdain
God's feet bore the brunt of the nails again
But the cry of God by God forsaken

Revolutionaries seek a god so tame
A lying utopia they pretend into birth
Choosing a god to suit their niggardly earth
Plucking him out from minds of no worth
A God himself in revolt is no way the same

The matter's too hard for a human to paint
Of all gods in the world under the sun
A god-atheist there can only be one
Whose God belief was for an instant undone
Becoming for atheists their own patron saint.

DOURO TRUCKS

Introduction

As a boy my family would go 'up the Douro' where the port vineyards were. I loved these trips. One of the most familiar sounds was the deep grinding of the wheels of the ox-carts as they made their way up narrow rocks and dust-strewn paths. They deliberatedly did not oil the wheels so that another ox-cart at the bottom or top of the path, which might be round a bend in the mountain, would know that another such vehicle was on the path so would wait until it had finished its journey. This might have taken as much as an hour and a half. Life was not so hectic in those days. To-day ordinary trucks wend their way up and down these mountain tracks and the poem was written watching one of them but with an eye to the past.

Douro trucks

Along a path on a hillside's back
A white truck stirs up swirling dust
Ploughing noiseless along the amber track
Curving the mountain's generous bust

Its whereabouts betrayed by a dusty wind
Fastens my eyes to its unknown destiny
Reaching the shoulder it's now hidden behind
Leaving a pillar of cloud - a relic for many.

Fifty years past the ears did pierce
A whining screech that hurts like sin
Making eyes search out this culprit fierce
Yoked mice making this fearful din?

The ancient oxen's heads in armour
Huge Catherine wheels revolving drily
Astride them rides a focussed farmer
The warrior sound clears the path entirely

SHAME

Introduction

Life is a marvellous gift. The sign that I forget it is shame. This short poem does not do justice to what shame reveals.

Shame

Into a world of wonder I was born
Slipped into life's living stream
Yet I complain grumpily every morn
That the world targets me with a darkened beam

My mother to me joyously attended
While pained by a tubercular knee
Yet my misfortune was all I minded
Demanding more be given to me

You may come to see me entirely free
'Do you not need your living to earn?'
'There is something more important to learn,
Have it for months, one, two, three.'

Yet I thought it was my right
A three month gift is mine for ever
'It's my right; a gift - never!'
The thought now makes my throat go tight.

I believed my being was all
I want to bury it now underground
So I'll never again hear its sound
It makes me now impossibly small

RICHARD

Introduction

On 17th May my friend, Richard Champion, died of cancer. In October of that year his widow, Rachel, organized a ceremonial burial of his ashes in the cemetery of the lovely church at Instow in north Devon. She asked me to speak at the graveside so I composed this poem and read it on that occasion.

Richard

Firmly standing in a tweed brown suit
A speech of passion on his open face
Selling ice-cream to innocent Welshmen
Unilever's rebel in that hideous brute.
Now his own spirit he gave and not sold
Catching my love which did quickly unfold.

Ignoring completely the smoke-filled chatter,
Of black cassocked figures encircling
This new boy in brown never minded
He had something to say which did matter
In my interested eye he could definitely see
He'd made for ever a good friend of me.

That Hertfordshire place was a seed-bed
Twin-yoked were we now in God's work
Heartened in zeal by a humane old Pope
This was our goal: Christ and the world to be wed
Richard's flame of devotion inspired all the youth
My own ardent yearning: to dig deep for truth.

Seated side-by-side in an echoing hall
Five years in love were we listening
To words both debased and sublime
Jonathan and David were together in thrall.
At hypocritical morals we silently winked
God's splendid embrace made us immortally linked.

One night together we looked up high
The empty vastness we stared at in wonder
Immensity's passion embracing our smallness
Staring at God's diamonds studding the sky.
Two friends were bonded by this infinite name
Keeping our love for ever the same.

This heavenly vision expanded our mind
Guiding us through the chaos of life
Our professions later different became
This infinite light our friendship did bind
The potter uniquely baking his clay
The analyst working in a new way

Out of this ivory cradle were thrown
Two priests to the docks of East London
We both could hear the sound of Bow Bells
Warm cockney bosoms took us as their own
One went to St. Catherine's in the parish of Bow
The other to Poplar - just a stone's throw.

An Angel from heaven had to Poplar descended
Stirring with marvel its stale old waters
A miracle spring sprung up in their place
Wounded souls therein were now mended
God's love lived now through youths who were jiving
A parish of bliss that was bubbling and thriving.

"I fear, Father, greatly my sin to confess
I had sex with my girl-friend on Saturday night"
In the midst of a dance spoke this timid teenager
Richard saw in his face a boy in distress.
"Your confession and sorrow has already been done,
You've spoken to me and I'll absolve you in one."

The boy he looked puzzled and Richard could see
He'd need to explain the spirit within
"I'm your priest sent by Jesus to you in this place
You've spoken in sorrow about it to me."
The boy looking could see a cross over his head
The dancing went on as forgiveness was said.

God who at Cana changed water to wine
Turning dense smog into glorious cloud
Those ancient feet treading in Poplar to-day
Are the same as had trod in old Palestine
Sent to those living in grief and dejection
A Richard that gave to them new direction.

Out of the Church he sped with new passion
Embracing the world in a woman called Rachel
Her womb came to bud with new life from his seed
Children came out in a generous ration
Released from the darkness into bright light
New lives that for him were a pure delight.

Friendship had reached its forty-sixth year
Sundered unfairly by cruel disease
Minding the death of a childhood Richard
A friend of my father's most cherished and dear
He was pierced in the heart by this lazer's ray
His son felt it not then, but does so to-day.

On 5th December I cannot now ring
No Richard to speak with now on the line
The day standing still as a silent tombstone
The date a great grief will always now bring
Saddest memory of my dearest old friend
My broken heart I just cannot mend.